The teacher

by Jenny Giles
Photography by Lynette Zeeng

I am at school
with my friends.

We are going
to see our teacher.

We go into the classroom,
and our teacher smiles at us.

We help her with the books.

In the morning,

we have our news time.

Our teacher talks to us,

and we talk to her.

She writes a story with us,

and we read it with her.

Today is Friday.
It is a sunny day.
We can see autumn leaves on the tre[e]
Th[ey are] red and yellow.
[Jack] has a new baby sister.
Jack's grandma is coming to visit.
We have a new
farm set in our room.

The Enormous
Watermelon

The Enormous
Watermelon

The Enormous
Watermelon

The Enormous
Watermelon

7 Seeds

The Enormous
Watermelon

The Enormous
Watermelon

The Enormous
Watermelon

animal toys

How Many?

Cars and Trucks

Soft Toys

Dol[ls]

I read my book to the teacher.

The teacher reads a story to us.

At recess,

we go outside.

We run and play games,

and our teacher looks after us.

After recess,

we run into the classroom.

Our teacher is not pleased,

and she stops us.

She says that someone will get hurt

if we run inside.

She makes us walk.

We do math at school.

The teacher helps us
with our work.

I am good at math.

After school,
Mom comes
to get me.
I wave
to my teacher,
and I go home.